Matilda learns a valuable lesson

by Holly-ann Martin

For my family, without whose life's lessons I wouldn't be who I am.

For all the children I have already taught Protective
Behaviours to, always remember these lessons and
may they continually keep you safe.

For all the children who have this story read to them,
may it help keep you safe.

Matilda was a very happy little girl who had two little sisters and a baby brother.

Everything was wonderful in Matilda's life. She felt safe all the time. Well, except for when her family went to visit Uncle Charlie and Aunty Rose.

Whenever Matilda and her family visited Uncle Charlie's home, she would start to feel sick. She hated going to his house. She knew, when it was time to leave, Uncle Charlie would scrape his whiskers down her face, then take out his false teeth and want to kiss her.

This really made Matilda feel unsafe. She did everything

to avoid going to Uncle Charlie and Aunty Rose's house.

Sometimes she would be naughty.

Sometimes she said she was feeling sick.

Sometimes she would even hide.

Nothing is so bad that we
can't talk with someone!

One day at school, Matilda's teacher, Miss Martin, told the class she was going to teach something called Protective Behaviours. She said it was about teaching children how to keep themselves safe. Miss Martin explained that sometimes grown ups weren't always there to keep them safe. "We're going to learn how to make good choices so you can keep yourself safe," said Miss Martin.

And then she continued. "You need to remember two very important things. The first is, 'We all have the right to feel safe all of the time.'" Matilda paid real attention because she knew that when she went to visit Uncle Charlie she didn't feel safe.

"The second is, 'We can talk with someone about anything.'" said Miss Martin. Well, Matilda wondered about this because she knew adults didn't always listen to kids or believe them. She was really interested to find out more.

Next, Miss Martin talked about something called Early Warning Signs. She had the whole class repeat the phrase after her as it was hard to say and no one knew what it meant. Miss Martin explained that Early Warning Signs were your body's way of telling you that you are getting a 'NO' feeling or were feeling unsafe. "It's that feeling you get when you feel like there are butterflies in your tummy, or maybe your legs feel like they are made of jelly or when your heart beats fast," she said.

As Miss Martin was talking, Matilda knew the feelings she got when she went to visit Uncle Charlie were her Early Warning Signs. It all made sense, but what could she do about it? Lastly, Miss Martin said that if you were getting your Early Warning Signs you have to tell someone on your Network. She explained that a network is a group of five people that you trust.

People in your network will listen to you, believe you and,
if necessary, take action to make you feel safe again. Miss
Martin helped the whole class make a Network. Matilda had
her Mum, Miss Martin and Mrs Bilney from school, Mrs Miller
from Brownies and her Aunty Rose on her Network.
She knew they would all listen, all believe, and help
her to feel safe.

Miss Martin also talked about something called 'persistence'.

Persistence means you keep trying, you never give up.

Grown ups may not always listen to children for all kinds of

reasons. So if this happens, you have to keep telling until

someone does listen and your Early Warning Signs go away.

This all made perfect sense to Matilda.

She knew what she had to do the next time her family went

to visit Uncle Charlie.

The next time Matilda's family went to visit Uncle Charlie and Aunty Rose she told her Mum she didn't like the way Uncle Charlie would scrape her face on his whiskers and then take out his teeth. Mum said, "Don't be silly, he is only playing."
It was not supposed to happen like this! Luckily, Miss Martin had told the class that not all adults listen to children, you have to persist, you have to keep telling until you feel safe again.

Matilda loved her Aunty Rose. She was another person on her Network. Matilda thought she would give it another try. Aunty Rose was outside taking in the washing, so Matilda went out to help and to have a chat with Aunty Rose. She told her how she felt when Uncle Charlie took out his teeth and tried to kiss her. She said it made her feel unsafe. "I love you both but I don't like visiting because of what Uncle Charlie does," said Matilda.

Aunty Rose listened to Matilda and told her how happy she was that Matilda had shared this with her.

Aunty Rose said Uncle Charlie thought he was just being funny, but she would talk to him in private and have him stop doing it. When Matilda and her family went to leave, Aunty Rose gave Matilda a big hug and Uncle Charlie gave her a cheeky wink. He never took his teeth out again.

She loves visiting Uncle Charlie and Aunty Rose now and always feels safe there.

Matilda always remembered the lesson that Miss Martin gave that day and she taught it to her sisters and her little brother.

A message to parents and teachers

This book was written to help teachers and parents talk with children about self protection in a gentle and meaningful way. Although it doesn't speak directly about unwanted sexual touching, children can still make connections to events and incidents in their own lives.

As adults we need to be careful about the messages we give to children. For instance, making a child kiss someone they don't feel comfortable with sends the message that they always have to do what an adult tells them to.

It is important to talk to children about:

FEELINGS: Teach children the names of emotions so that they can recognise and express how they are feeling. As adults, we need to accept how children feel and avoid discounting their feelings by saying things like don't be scared, don't be silly, etc.

EARLY WARNING SIGNS: These are involuntary physical sensations that our bodies experience when we do not feel safe, when we are excited or when we are in challenging situations. It's our natural "fight or flight" response to a perceived danger. Early warning signs are specific to the individual and we each experience them differently. For example, some may get butterflies in their tummies, while others may get sweaty palms and a dry throat.

NETWORKS: Help children develop a Network of five trusted adults to whom they can tell anything. These people will provide support and protect them.

PERSISTENCE: This is a crucial aspect of Protective Behaviours as children may not always be believed or may still have their Early Warning Signs after telling an adult they feel unsafe. Children must be encouraged to keep telling and keep telling until they feel safe or until their Early Warning Signs go away.

PUBLIC AND PRIVATE: It is very important that children be taught the correct names for their private body parts and that 'private' means just for them. Private body parts are those parts of the body covered by bathers and also include the mouth. Reinforce with children that they own their body and no one should touch any part of them without their permission.

SAYING "NO": Children need to know that they can say "No" to anybody, even adults, if they feel unsafe or if they have their Early Warning Signs. Children need to learn to say "No" assertively. This is done by looking the person in the eye and saying "No" as if they really mean it. Also teach children that sometimes it might be necessary to use an Emergency "NO" if they are in real danger.

SECRETS: Children need to know that there are two kinds of secrets. Good secrets will make somebody happy when the secret is revealed and are only kept for a short time.

Bad secrets will make them feel unsafe and they will be told they must never tell; the secret must be kept for ever and ever, maybe a whole lifetime. Children need to be told that they never need to keep bad secrets.

With a bad secret, children may get their Early Warning Signs. They must never keep Bad Secrets and should be encouraged to tell someone on their Network. Other ways children can identify a Bad Secret is that there may only be two people who know the secret. Teach children they should never have to keep a secret about any kind of touching, even if they like the touch or the secret little special game.

RECEIVING A DISCLOSURE:

If your child discloses that they have been abused, either physically, sexually or emotionally, here are some suggestions which may help your child, and you, to feel safe:

- Stay calm.
- Try to put your feelings aside as an angry reaction will only make your child feel like they shouldn't have disclosed.
- Believe your child.
- Kids rarely lie about abuse. They are often discouraged from disclosing because they think no-one will believe them. It's really important that they know you believe them.
- Offer reassurance.
- Keep telling your child that it is not their fault and they haven't done anything wrong, they are not to blame. Use words such as: "I'm really pleased you told me." "You've done the right thing by telling someone on your Network." Or "I'm sorry this has happened to you but we'll work this out together."
- Make no promises.
- Do not promise to keep this a secret, use Protective Behaviours language to explain that you will have to tell someone on your Network.
- Contact authorities.
  - The Department for Child Protection.
  - Police Child Protection Unit.
  - Crimestoppers.

Do not pressure your child to give full details, they may have to repeat their story for the police or doctors and they may find it hard each time to have to recount what has happened to them.

Do not approach the perpetrator yourself, leave this to the authorities.

© 2011 Holly-ann Martin
First published 2011

Author: Holly-ann Martin
Illustrations: Marilyn Fahie
Design: traceygibbs.com

Safe4Kids Pty Ltd
PO Box 367
Armadale 6992
Western Australia

www.safe4kids.com.au

National Library of Australia Cataloguing-in-Publication entry

Author: Martin, Holly-Ann.

Title: Matilda learns a valuable lesson / Holly-Ann Martin ;
illustrator, Marilyn Fahie.

Edition: 1st ed.

ISBN: 9780980529432 (hbk.)

Target Audience: For primary school age.

Subjects: Child abuse--Prevention--Juvenile literature.

Other Authors/Contributors: Fahie, Marilyn.

Dewey Number: 362.7672

ISBN: 978-0-9805294-3-2

Printed in China
Hung Hing Off-Set Printing Co, Ltd